WAVES
and
INFORMATION
TRANSFER

Heather C. Hudak

 Crabtree Publishing Company
www.crabtreebooks.com

Crabtree Publishing Company

www.crabtreebooks.com

Author: Heather Hudak

Series research and development: Reagan Miller

Editorial director: Kathy Middleton

Editor: Janine Deschenes

Proofreaders: Ellen Rodger and Petrice Custance

Design: Ken Wright

Cover design: Ken Wright

Photo research: Heather Hudak, Ken Wright

Production coordinator and
    Prepress technician: Ken Wright

Print coordinator: Margaret Amy Salter

Animation and digital resources produced for
Crabtree Publishing by Plug-In Media

Photo Credits:
Wikimedia: p17 (top left); p28 (right)

All other images from Shutterstock

Library and Archives Canada Cataloguing in Publication

Hudak, Heather C., 1975-, author
    Waves and information transfer / Heather Hudak.

(Catch a wave)
Includes index.
Issued in print and electronic formats.
ISBN 978-0-7787-2962-4 (hardcover).--
ISBN 978-0-7787-2970-9 (paperback).--
ISBN 978-1-4271-1857-8 (HTML)

    1. Waves--Juvenile literature. 2. Sound-waves--Juvenile literature.
3. Light--Wave-length--Juvenile literature. 4. Wave theory of light--Juvenile
literature. 5. Carrier waves--Juvenile literature. I. Title.

QC157.H82 2017   j531'.1133   C2016-907056-5
                               C2016-907057-3

Library of Congress Cataloging-in-Publication Data

Names: Hudak, Heather C., 1975- author.
Title: Waves and information transfer / Heather Hudak.
Description: New York, New York : Crabtree Publishing Company, [2017] |
  Series: Catch a wave | Includes index.
Identifiers: LCCN 2016059052 (print) | LCCN 2016059910 (ebook) |
  ISBN 9780778729624 (reinforced library binding) |
  ISBN 9780778729709 (pbk.) |
  ISBN 9781427118578 (Electronic HTML)
Subjects: LCSH: Electromagnetic waves--Juvenile literature. | Wave
  mechanics--Juvenile literature. | Information technology--Juvenile
  literature.
Classification: LCC QC661 .H785 2017 (print) | LCC QC661 (ebook) | DDC
  530.12/4--dc23
LC record available at https://lccn.loc.gov/2016059052

Crabtree Publishing Company

www.crabtreebooks.com   1-800-387-7650

Printed in Canada/032017/BF20170111

Published in Canada
Crabtree Publishing
616 Welland Ave.
St. Catharines, Ontario
L2M 5V6

Published in the United States
Crabtree Publishing
PMB 59051
350 Fifth Avenue, 59th Floor
New York, New York 10118

Published in the United Kingdom
Crabtree Publishing
Maritime House
Basin Road North, Hove
BN41 1WR

Published in Australia
Crabtree Publishing
3 Charles Street
Coburg North
VIC, 3058

CONTENTS

WAVES in MOTION

When you think of waves, you probably think of waves that surfers ride in the ocean. But water waves are just one type of wave. Light waves create the colors you see with your eyes. Sound waves make the sounds you hear with your ears. Waves are **vibrations** or **disturbances** that travel through a **medium** or an empty space. They transfer, or move, energy from one place to another in regular **patterns**.

HOW ARE WAVES MADE?

Matter is anything that takes up space and has **mass**. Mass is the amount of material in an object. Orange juice, your television, and the air around you are all forms of matter. When a force is applied to matter, it vibrates. This changes the matter from its rest position by making it move up and down or side to side. This creates waves. Waves carry energy from the force. They travel away from the source in the form of a wave. The matter returns to its original position once the energy passes through it. When the waves run out of energy, they stop moving.

When you knock on a door, the place you hit **vibrates**. The vibration makes the air around the door vibrate, too. The sound waves created by the vibrations carry the knocking sound to your ears. When you stop knocking, the vibrations stop, too. Without vibrations, there are no sound waves. You stop hearing the sound.

WAVES TRANSFER INFORMATION

There are many types of waves that transfer energy. But did you know that some waves can also transfer information from one place to another? Information is any type of data that can be put into a message or observed, such as phone calls or text messages. Telephones, televisions, and radios all use waves to send and receive information.

PATTERNS of INFORMATION

Waves are regular patterns of motion. They have specific **properties** that create patterns of movement. These properties include amplitude, wavelength, and frequency.

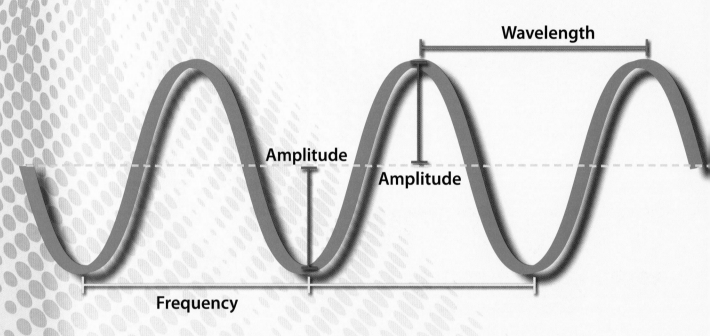

Amplitude is the height of a wave from its center, or resting point, to its tallest point, or crest. It can also be measured from the resting point to its lowest point, or trough.

Wavelength is the length from one point on a wave to the same point on the next wave. It is usually measured from crest to crest or trough to trough.

Frequency is the number of waves that pass through a certain place in a specific period of time.

TYPES of WAVES

There are two types of wave patterns: **transverse** and **longitudinal**. Transverse waves move up and down. Think of a rope tied to a tree. If you move the free end of the rope up and down, you can make a transverse wave.

Longitudinal waves move horizontally, or from side to side. If you move a Slinky toy back and forth, you are representing the movement of a longitudinal wave.

Transverse wave

Longitudinal wave

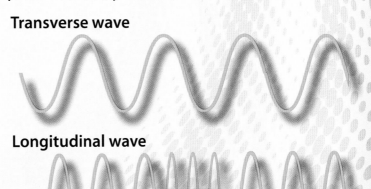

COMMUNICATING INFORMATION

Waves are repeating patterns. A pattern is anything that regularly happens over and over again. We can predict and interpret patterns, and use them to **communicate**.

     Some patterns are easy to see. We know the sun rises in the east and sets in the west each day. Using the alphabet, we create patterns of letters that form words and phrases. Other patterns use codes and symbols that we need to interpret. In order to decode the pattern, both the sender and the **receiver** need to know the code. To decode means to figure out the meaning of a coded message. Can you figure out the code used to write this sentence?

Eht yks si eulb.

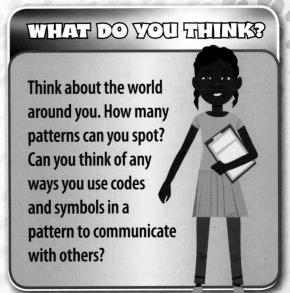

WHAT DO YOU THINK?

Think about the world around you. How many patterns can you spot? Can you think of any ways you use codes and symbols in a pattern to communicate with others?

INFORMATION WAVES

Waves help us communicate with each other. But transferring information is not as simple as putting a message in a bottle so it can ride the ocean waves until it washes ashore. Information transfer is much more complicated, and it involves both light and sound waves. Your ears, eyes, and brain work together to **interpret** the patterns of waves so you can see and hear information.

Traffic lights are one way people communicate using light waves. Each one has a red, yellow, and green light. They signal to drivers when they should stop, slow down, or move forward.

COMMUNICATING WITH LIGHT

Lighthouses are tall, circular towers with a bright light at the top. The light shines in the dark to let sailors know their ships are near the shoreline. They are one way that people use light waves to communicate—and stay safe!

SENDING SIGNALS WITH SOUND

Have you ever heard a thunder clap? It tells you a storm is coming. A doorbell ringing, a baby crying, or a text pinging are just a few of the sounds you hear every day. They communicate messages about what is going on in your environment.

WHAT DO YOU THINK?

What sounds can you hear right now? Close your eyes and listen closely. Think about the ways you can learn about what is going on around you by interpreting the sounds you hear. What types of sounds can you make to communicate with others?

People use many different sounds to communicate. Your voice is a sound that you use to speak or sing. The sound of a siren blaring sends the message that there is an emergency. Instruments, such as drums, can send information through sound waves. Your ears interpret that information as music.

WAVES in TIME

For thousands of years, people have used light and sound waves to communicate. Long before we had telephones, **satellites**, and the Internet, people found creative ways to send messages to each other using waves.

Around 1800 B.C., soldiers along the Great Wall of China used smoke signals to warn of enemy attacks. Towers were set up along the wall, and soldiers would relay these smoke messages from one tower to the next.

UP in FLAMES

One way early people communicated over long distances was with smoke **signals**. A signal is a message or method to communicate a message. By using fire to create smoke, people could send coded messages to each other through light waves, which allowed people to see the smoke. Smoke signals were important ways of communicating. For example, one puff might warn of danger, while two puffs may communicate that all is safe.

TAP IT OUT

Fast forward hundreds of years to the 1800s, when a man named Samuel Morse forever changed the way people communicate. He found a way to send **electrical** signals over a wire from one place to another. Then he came up with a system of dots and dashes to represent each letter of the alphabet. It was called Morse code. In 1844, Morse sent his first message. He used flashing lights and clicking sounds to symbolize each dot and dash. Wires were set up across the country so people could send messages to each other. Both the machine and the messages that came from them were called telegraphs

This is an early machine that can tap out and send messages in Morse Code. It is called a straight key.

MODERN-DAY MORSE CODE

Morse code is rarely used today. Throughout the 1900s, inventors came up with new **technologies** to help us communicate over long distances using light, sound, and other types of waves. Telephones, satellites, and the Internet are just a few examples. What other communication technologies can you think of? How do they use patterns and codes to send messages?

11

LOOKING for NEW SOLUTIONS

Early forms of communication had some major challenges. People were limited in the types of messages they could send. After all, you can only say so much with a puff of smoke, and interpreting dots and dashes took time. People wanted faster, better ways to communicate. Luckily, technology is always changing and improving. Each day, engineers find new ways to do things. Engineers are people who use math and science to design **devices** that solve problems, such as sending messages quickly and easily. Some engineers design patterns using light and sound waves. They use these patterns to find better ways for people to communicate.

Engineers have updated and improved radio technology many times over the past 100 years.

RADIO WAVES

Radio waves are a form of **electromagnetic wave** best known for their role in communication. Electromagnetic waves do not need to pass through a medium and can travel through empty space. They were first discovered in the late 1800s. Not long after, a man named Heinrich Hertz realized he could use radio waves to send and receive messages.

Students are pictured here, in 1912, practicing how to send and receive telegraphs at the Marconi wireless school in New York City.

In the 1890s, Guglielmo Marconi invented a device that used radio waves to send and receive messages in the form of coded signals. They were known as wireless telegraphs. Nearly 30 years later, he adapted his device to **transmit** voices and music. We know these devices as radios. Over the years, engineers have found even more new ways to use radio waves. In fact, objects you use every day, such as televisions and cell phones, use radio waves.

INNOVATIONS in WAVE TECHNOLOGY

Over time, engineers found innovative ways to use light and sound waves for communicating information. For example, doctors use ultrasound technology to learn about what is going on inside the human body. Ultrasound is a type of sound wave made by electrical equipment. The wave vibrates at a very high frequency. Doctors run special scanners over the skin, which send beams of ultrasound waves into the body. The waves bounce off bones, organs, and tissues. They send signals to a computer that interprets the information into a picture.

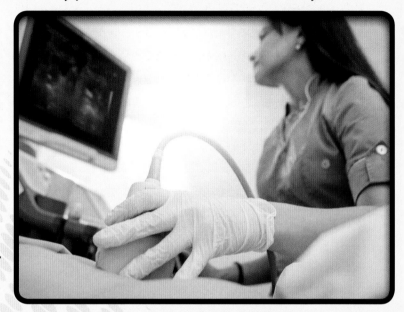

ECHO in the OCEAN

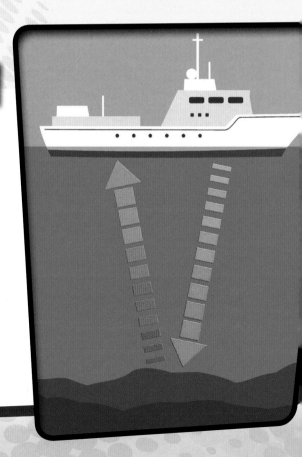

Sound waves can also be used to draw pictures of other things we cannot see with our eyes. Parts of the ocean are too deep for humans to explore. Instead, people use **sonar** to find out what the ocean floor looks like. Sonar is a technique that involves sending sound waves deep into the water. When they hit the bottom of the ocean, they bounce back, or echo. The echoes carry information about surfaces and objects, allowing us to draw a map of the ocean floor.

WIRELESS WAVES

Imagine you needed to be connected to all of the other computers or cell phones in the world in order to send and receive messages. At one time, you needed to be connected via **cables** to send a message to a person in a faraway place. Televisions and telephones both relied on cables to receive information from satellites and **antennae**. Today, most connections are wireless.

Radio waves carry signals directly to cell phones, televisions, and computers. Internet Wi-Fi works the same way. Your modem sends and receives radio waves wirelessly using a special computer language. Your computer translates the language into the images and words you see onscreen.

LIVING in a DIGITAL WORLD

Data is any information a person or machine can understand and interpret, such as videos, music, and pictures. It is transmitted from one place to another on waves. First, data is converted into signals. Signals are transmitted along a path, such as a wave. Digital signals are a pattern, or sequence, of numbers, letters, and characters that computers can process. Most digital signals use binary code.

BINARY CODE in ACTION

Binary code is all around us. It is found in electronic devices such as microwave ovens, portable music players, and light switches. This is because electronic devices can only understand two states: on or off. Binary code lets us use these two states to communicate messages. In binary code, the state of being on is represented by the number one. The number zero represents the state of being off. Digital information is any image, sound, document, or signal made using binary code. Using binary code, people can transfer digital information from one device to another. Each letter of the alphabet is assigned a sequence of eight numbers using binary code. For example, A is written 01000001.

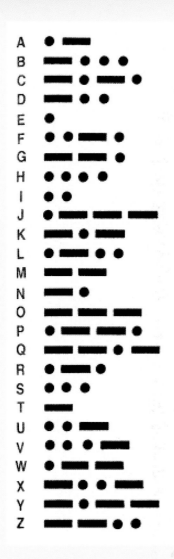

BACK in TIME

Morse code works much like binary code. Each letter of the alphabet is represented by a pattern of dashes and dots, like the ones shown to the left.

The message sender uses a special device to tap out a message of dots and dashes. The tapping turns the electrical current on or off, creating pulses. On the other end of the line, the receiving device takes in the pattern of pulses and writes them down as dots and dashes on a piece of paper. The person receiving the message then uses the special code to spell out the words.

When sailors at sea were in trouble, they would tap out a simple message that was easy to interpret. Can you read the message using the code?

● ● ● ▬▬ ▬▬ ▬▬ ● ● ●

People used machines such as these to listen to messages. Then, they would decode them.

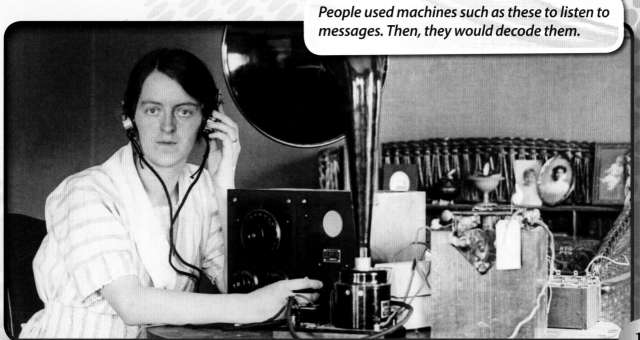

DIGITIZING the DATA AROUND US

Have you ever played a game of telephone? You sit in a circle with a large group of friends, whispering a message from one person to the next. The last person reveals the message, and most often it sounds nothing like the words that came from the first person in the circle. Digital information transfer helps keep the message from losing its meaning.

When you get a phone call from a friend, do you trust that the words you hear are the same ones your friend is saying on the other end? Of course you do. Engineers have found reliable ways to transmit sound and light waves over long distances. It is the same when you send a text or email message. You know the words you write will be the same ones that appear for the person you sent them to.

Transmitting Texts

Over the past 100 years, the technology people use to send and receive messages has changed, but the basic ideas behind information transfer are the same. Today, people have a modern kind of Morse code. Text messages work in a similar way. You tap out a message on your cell phone using numbers and letters. The computer circuits inside your phone turn each letter into binary code. Using waves, the code is sent to the receiver. That person's phone converts the code into the words that appear in the text message.

WHAT DO YOU THINK?

Now that you know waves are converted into digital signals, what ways can you think of to transfer digital information? What types of digital signals do you use each day in your own life?

WAVES and YOUR DEVICES

Do you like to talk on the phone with your friends? Each time you have a conversation on the phone, you are transferring information from one place to another. To do this, you need to send and receive different kinds of signals.

When you speak into the microphone on your telephone, sound waves vibrate through the phone in the form of radio waves. The vibrations made by your voice are a smooth, **continuous** wave. To be continuous means to go on without being stopped. This type of wave changes amplitude and frequency to match the voice or sound being transmitted.

In order to transfer information through the phone to your friend, the signals from your voice are converted into digital signals. Digital signals are not continuous. They turn sound, such as your voice, into binary code. The code is sent to another device that interprets the code. It reassembles the original signal so your friend can hear the sound of your voice.

Just like the phone example, the same thing happens when you watch television or use the Internet. A message is sent from a transmitter, such as a satellite or computer. Some sort of hardware or device converts the message into a digital signal made of binary code. The signal transmits to a receiver, where it is decoded and converted back into the original message.

WIRELESS WAVES

Have you ever seen towers with lines running from one tower to the next along the side of the road? In the past, people used physical cables to send and receive data using signals. Electromagnetic waves carried signals across the cables.

In some parts of the world, we still need cables to send messages. In many places, we use wireless communications. Electromagnetic waves carry digital signals using antennae instead. Electromagnetic signals radiate from the antenna. The signals are then picked up by a receiving antenna, which converts the signals into the original message.

Antennae come in many sizes, depending on wavelength and frequency. Higher frequency waves have a shorter wavelength. They need a shorter antenna. Lower frequency waves have longer wavelengths and require a taller antenna.

Wireless Phone Calls

A cell phone communicates through a base station. A radio tower at the station sends and receives signals to and from your phone. As you move out of your tower's range, your cell service is passed on to the next tower and so on. Instead of losing the signal, it travels with you.

WIRELESS WAVELENGTHS

Wireless communications use three basic types of electromagnetic waves. Radio waves have a low frequency and can travel long distances. They carry signals for devices such as cordless phones, radios, televisions, garage door openers, GPS, and radio-controlled cars.

Microwaves can also travel long distances. They are used to transmit information from Bluetooth devices, cell phones, and satellites.

Infrared waves carry large amounts of data but have a limited range. They are perfect for short-range communication. They carry data from a remote control to a television, a mouse to a computer, or a computer to a printer.

WHAT DO YOU THINK?

Do you have a cell phone? What kinds of waves does it use to send and receive messages? How are they sent over long distances? Describe the process.

SENDING MESSAGES WITH WAVES

Did you know you can create waves that communicate information using just a flashlight? It can be as simple as using pulses of light to send a message. As long as both the sender and receiver both know the code, they can interpret the message

Experiment

How can you communicate using binary code?

Materials

- 2 flashlights
- Paper and pen

Procedure

1. Form a group of four people.
2. Discuss binary code and how you can use it to send messages with flashlights. Consider the state of being on as the number one and the state of being off as zero.
3. Think about how you can communicate words using binary code. For example, the letter A may be equal to the number one, while the letter B is equal to zero.
4. Split into two teams of two, and make sure each team has a flashlight.
5. Each team will write down a pattern of As and Bs that they can communicate using their flashlights. Be sure to keep the pattern a secret from the other team.
6. The first team will turn the flashlight on and off to send their pattern using pulses of light. The second team will write down what they saw using the letters A and B.
7. Reverse roles, and repeat the experiment.
8. Discuss your results. Did each team get the pattern right? What challenges did you face?

What Happened and Why?

Binary code helped each team communicate a simple pattern using pulses of light.

CREATE YOUR OWN CODE

What if you had your own secret language to communicate with your friends? You could send and receive messages without anyone else knowing what they mean. You can use light or sound waves to communicate your messages.

Experiment

Using symbols and waves to communicate words.

Materials

- A copy of Morse code (see pg 17 or 28)
- 2 sheets of paper
- 2 pens
- 2 flashlights
- 2 whistles

Procedure

1. Get in a group of four people.
2. Look at the copy of Morse code on page 17. How is each letter made using sound or light waves? How is Morse code an example of binary code?
3. Make your own code using signals that represent "on" or "off," similar to the dots and dashes in Morse code or ones and zeros of binary code.
4. Make sure each member of your group writes the code on a separate sheet of paper.
5. Now that you have created your secret code, try using your flashlights to send and receive messages.
6. Break into groups of two, and have one group stand on each side of the table.
7. Take turns sending messages using your secret code. Start with a simple word, and try making your message more complex every time you try it.
8. Talk to your group members. Does the code work? Did the other team decode your message?
9. Find a way to improve your code, or make it easier to understand. Now, try asking each other questions and give answers using the code. How does your improved code compare to your old one?
10. Now, repeat steps 6 through 9 using the whistles instead of the flashlights. Be sure to change the messages you send.
11. How are your results different? How were they the same? Which tool was easier to use, the flashlight or the whistle? Why?

What if you had to communicate your secret code over a long distance or through obstacles? Do you think sound waves or light waves will work better to send your message?

Experiment

Using symbols and waves to communicate words.

Materials

- A copy of Morse code
- 2 sheets of paper
- 2 pens
- 2 flashlights
- 2 whistles

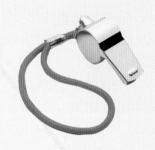

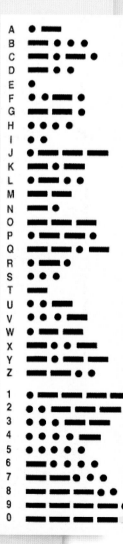

Procedure

1. Choose the code from the previous experiment that works best. After the sun goes down, go with a friend and two adults to a large outdoor area, such as a soccer field.
2. Break into groups of one adult and one child, and walk as far away from each other as possible. Once you are at each end of the field, you need to find a way to send each other a coded message. Which tool will work best to send a message over a long distance?
3. Take turns sending messages using your secret code and the flashlights. Are you able to see the lights?
4. Next, try sending each other messages using your secret code and the whistles. Can you hear the whistles blow?
5. Once each group has successfully decoded at least two messages, come back together to discuss your results.
6. Next, move to a nearby building, such as your home. Have one group go inside and the other group stand outside. Which tool will work best to send a message through an obstacle, such as a wall?
7. Try sending coded messages through using your flashlights first and then the whistles.
8. What happens now? Write down your results. What if you only had a flashlight?

What Happened and Why?

Using flashlights and whistles, you were able to send coded messages over long distances and through obstacles using both light and sound waves. By turning the lights on or off or blowing into the whistles, you created patterns of signals that your team members were able to interpret. In this way, waves communicated information to you.

Record the findings of your experiments. Be sure to include the answers to the following questions.

1. How did you use your flashlight to communicate information using light waves?
2. What problems did you encounter? Were you able to see the light over a long distance? What do you think would happen if you tried the experiment in daylight?
3. How did you use your whistle to communicate information using sound waves?
4. What problems did you encounter? Were you able to hear the whistle over a long distance? Were there other sounds that made it difficult to hear? How could you have improved your sound?
5. What happened when one group moved indoors? Did you encounter any problems? Was it easier to send messages using light or sound waves?
6. Compare the different types of patterns, or "codes," you sent. Which ones worked best to transmit information? Why?

Share your results with other groups. How were their findings similar or different? What worked well for them that you could use to improve your own results?

Further Reading

Sound Waves and Communication (Science Readers: Content and Literacy). Jenna Winterberg. Teacher Created Materials, 2015.

Waves of Light and Sound (Let's Explore Science). Shirley Duke. Rourke Educational Media, 2014.

Why Does Sound Travel?: All about Sound (Solving Science Mysteries (Paperback). Nicolas Brasch. PowerKids Press, 2010.

Websites

PBS Learning Media: The Electromagnetic Spectrum
Watch this video from NASA to learn all about electromagnetic waves.
http://bit.ly/1Z6P13z

GCSE Bitesize: Sound and Light
Learn more about the science of sound and light waves.
http://bbc.in/1o7ZfAq

For fun wave challenges, activities, and more, enter the code at the Crabtree Plus website below.

www.crabtreeplus.com/waves

Your code is:
caw17

Glossary

Some **boldfaced** words are defined where they appear in text.

antenna Wire that uses electromagnetic waves to transmit information

cable A bundle of wires in a rope-like formation that are used to connect things

communicate To share ideas and information

devices Tools that are used to perform tasks

disturbances Actions that interrupt an object from its resting place

electrical To do with the science of electric currents and charges

interpret To read or give meaning to something

medium Something that is used to carry or transmit something else, such as a signal

pattern Something that repeats

properties The essential or basic qualities of something

receiver A device that converts incoming waves into information

satellite A human-made object that circles around Earth and contains electrical devices for sending and receiving signals

sonar A tool and a method used to detect objects under water

technologies New tools or objects designed to solve problems and make life easier

transmit To pass or carry something from one place to another place

vibrations Actions that cause something to move back and forth quickly

Index